Innovative Jobscapes

Navigating New Frontiers in Employment

Written by

Morgan E. Blake

Independently published

2024

For permission requests, write to the publisher, addressed "Attention: Permissions Coordinator," at the address below.

info@socialized.cloud

Published by Morgan E. Blake

Book Layout ©2024 Morgan E. Blake

Cover Design ©2024 Morgan E. Blake

ISBN: 9798879107593

First Printing, 2024

Introduction: The Dawn of Innovative Jobscapes

Setting the Scene for Innovation

As we stand on the precipice of a new era in employment, it's essential to recognize the transformative forces at play that are reshaping the very fabric of how we work, seek jobs, and envision our careers. The landscape of employment is undergoing a seismic shift, propelled by a confluence of technological advancements, changing societal norms, and a global economy that's more interconnected than ever before. This chapter, *Setting the Scene for Innovation*, delves deep into these dynamics, laying the groundwork for understanding the monumental changes sweeping across the job market.

The inception of the digital age marked a pivotal turning point in human history, akin to the industrial revolution in its scope and impact. However, unlike any transformation witnessed in the past, the speed at which technology evolves today is unprecedented. This rapid pace of innovation has not only altered the tools we use but fundamentally changed the nature of work itself. From automation and artificial intelligence to the rise of the gig economy and remote work, the traditional paradigms of employment are being dismantled and reimagined.

In this dawn of innovative jobscapes, the concept of a 'job for life' has become an anachronism. The linear career paths that defined previous generations are giving way to more fluid and dynamic trajectories. Today, it's not uncommon for individuals to switch careers multiple times, embracing the opportunities and challenges that come with a constantly evolving job market. This fluidity is not just a response to the changing nature of jobs but also a reflection of a broader societal shift towards valuing diversity in experiences and skills.

Digital networking has emerged as a cornerstone of modern job hunting, transforming the way we connect with potential employers, colleagues, and collaborators. Platforms like LinkedIn, Twitter, and even industry-specific forums have become the new town squares of professional networking, enabling connections that were once constrained by geography or serendipity. In this digital arena, your online presence—your personal brand—plays a crucial role in how you are perceived professionally. It's a space where the content you create, the thoughts you share, and the networks you build can significantly influence your career opportunities.

Simultaneously, we're witnessing the ascent of the **gig economy**—a paradigm that champions flexibility, autonomy, and the freedom to choose when, where, and how to work. This shift towards freelance, contract, and temporary positions is redefining the employer-employee relationship, presenting both opportunities and challenges. On one hand, it offers unprecedented freedom and control over one's career; on the other, it demands a new set of skills and attitudes towards job security and career planning.

The concept of **remote work**, once a perk offered by a select few companies, has now become a mainstream mode of employment across various industries. Propelled further by global events and technological advancements, remote work has proven that productivity is not tethered to a physical office space. This transition to a more flexible work environment has opened up a global talent pool, allowing individuals to work for companies thousands of miles away without ever leaving their homes.

As we navigate through these innovative jobscapes, it's imperative to understand that with change comes uncertainty. The rise of **artificial intelligence and automation** presents a dual-edged sword; while they offer incredible efficiencies and new opportunities, they also pose significant challenges to job security and the nature of work itself. The key to thriving in this new era is adaptability—embracing lifelong learning, upskilling, and reskilling to remain relevant in an ever-changing job market.

This chapter sets the stage for a deep dive into each of these areas, exploring how they are reshaping the job market and what it means for job seekers, employees, and entrepreneurs alike. As we delve into the nuances of these innovative jobscapes, remember that with every challenge comes opportunity. The future of work is not a distant reality; it's unfolding here and now, and it beckons us to engage with it proactively, creatively, and with an open mind.

Understanding the Shift in Employment Paradigms

In navigating the contours of today's job market, one cannot help but observe the profound transformations that have redefined what it means to work, to seek employment, and to forge a career in the modern age. The narrative of employment has been rewritten, urging us to *understand the shift in employment paradigms* with a keen eye and an open mind. This chapter is a deep dive into the heart of these changes, examining the undercurrents that have propelled us into new realms of professional engagement.

The cornerstone of this shift is the transition from the industrial to the digital era, a leap that has not only introduced new technologies but has also reshaped the socio-economic landscapes in which we operate. The digital revolution has democratized information, decentralized job opportunities, and has led to the rise of knowledge work as a dominant form of employment. This transition is not merely about the tools we use but about a fundamental change in the nature of work itself.

In this new era, the traditional employment model—characterized by long-term, stable job engagements within hierarchical organizations—is increasingly giving way to more fluid and dynamic work arrangements. This shift is driven by several key factors, including technological advancements, globalization, and changing worker preferences, especially among younger generations who value flexibility, autonomy, and purpose in their careers.

The Gig Economy has emerged as a defining feature of this new employment paradigm. Characterized by freelance, contract, and temporary work, the gig economy offers both opportunities and challenges. On one hand, it provides workers with unprecedented freedom to choose when, where, and how they work. On the other hand, it presents new challenges related to job security, benefits, and long-term career development.

Remote Work, once a niche option, has become a mainstream choice for many, further illustrating the shift in employment paradigms. Enabled by digital technologies, remote work has dismantled geographical barriers, allowing individuals to work for companies across the globe without relocating. This has profound implications for how organizations manage their workforce, how teams collaborate, and how work-life balance is achieved.

Another critical aspect of this shift is the role of **Artificial Intelligence (AI) and Automation** in shaping the future of work. While these technologies promise to increase efficiency and open up new possibilities, they also raise important questions about the displacement of jobs and the skills workers need to remain relevant.

In response to these changes, there is a growing emphasis on **Upskilling and Reskilling**. The rapidly evolving job market demands that individuals continuously update their skills and knowledge to keep pace with new technologies and work practices. This lifelong learning approach is becoming essential for career resilience and growth.

Furthermore, the rise of **Digital Networking and Personal Branding** has transformed the way individuals seek and secure employment. In a world where opportunities are increasingly found and forged online, the ability to effectively present oneself and connect with others digitally has become a crucial skill set.

As we delve into these evolving paradigms, it becomes clear that the future of work is not a distant horizon but a present reality. The changes we are witnessing are not merely trends but represent a fundamental shift in how we conceive of work, employment, and career development. This chapter aims to equip you with the insights and understanding necessary to navigate this new landscape, not just as a participant but as a proactive architect of your own career path.

In charting this terrain, I draw upon my extensive research, practical experience, and the collective wisdom of professionals across various industries. The goal is to offer a compass for navigating the complexities of the modern job market, providing a clear-eyed view of the challenges and opportunities that lie ahead. By embracing these shifts, we can unlock new potentials and pathways, paving the way for a future of work that is more flexible, inclusive, and aligned with our evolving aspirations and values.

Chapter 1: The Evolution of the Job Market

Historical Perspectives on Employment

To truly grasp the essence of today's job market and the innovative landscapes that define it, it's imperative to journey back through the corridors of time and explore the *historical perspectives on employment*. This exploration is not just an academic exercise but a necessary voyage to understand the roots from which our current employment paradigms have evolved.

The story of employment is, in many ways, the story of civilization itself. From the agrarian societies that marked the dawn of human settlements to the complex digital economies of the 21st century, the way people work has always been a mirror reflecting the technological, social, and economic contours of their times.

In the earliest societies, work was primarily about survival. It was deeply intertwined with the rhythms of nature, and the division of labor was based more on physical capabilities and age than on any formalized skill set. As civilizations advanced, so did the complexity of work, giving rise to artisans, traders, and a more structured form of labor allocation.

The Industrial Revolution marked a seismic shift in the employment landscape. The introduction of machinery and the factory system transformed not only how work was done but also the very fabric of society. It ushered in an era of mass employment, standardized work hours, and a new urban working class. The assembly line became the symbol of this era, epitomizing efficiency and productivity, albeit at the cost of individual craftsmanship and, often, worker satisfaction.

Fast forward to the 20th century, and we witness the rise of the service sector and the knowledge worker, as coined by Peter Drucker. This period saw a significant shift from manual labor to work that valued intellectual skills and education. The advent of computers and the internet towards the latter part of the century set the stage for another monumental shift - the Digital Revolution.

The Digital Revolution has redefined the concept of work in unprecedented ways. It has blurred the boundaries between personal and professional life, between physical office spaces and virtual work environments. It has democratized access to information, breaking down geographical barriers and creating a global workforce.

In reflecting on these historical shifts, it becomes evident that each major transition brought with it challenges and opportunities. The Industrial Revolution, for instance, led to significant socio-economic changes, including urbanization and the rise of labor unions. It sparked debates about worker rights, job security, and the ethical implications of mechanization - themes that resonate even in today's discussions about automation and AI.

Similarly, the rise of the knowledge worker and the service economy brought to the fore the importance of education, lifelong learning, and adaptability. It highlighted the value of soft skills, such as communication, problem-solving, and emotional intelligence, which continue to be crucial in the digital age.

As we stand at the cusp of what many are calling the Fourth Industrial Revolution, marked by AI, robotics, and unprecedented digital connectivity, it's crucial to draw lessons from the past. Understanding the historical trajectories of employment helps contextualize the current shifts we're experiencing and provides a lens through which to anticipate future changes.

This chapter, therefore, is not just a look back but a bridge to understanding the present and future jobscapes. It's a reminder that while the tools, technologies, and terminologies of work may change, the underlying human needs for purpose, engagement, and fulfillment remain constant. By appreciating the historical contexts of employment, we're better equipped to navigate the innovative jobscapes of today and tomorrow, embracing the changes with insight and readiness for the opportunities they bring.

The Digital Revolution and Its Impact

As we delve into the transformative era known as the Digital Revolution, it's essential to recognize this period not just as a chapter in the annals of technology, but as a pivotal moment that has redefined the very essence of employment, career development, and the job market at large. This revolution, characterized by the rapid advancement of digital technology, has catalyzed profound changes in how we work, where we work, and the skills we need to thrive in the modern workplace.

At the heart of the Digital Revolution is the advent of the internet and the proliferation of digital devices, which have democratized information access and transformed global communication. This digital connectivity has erased geographical boundaries, creating a global marketplace and a virtual workspace that operates 24/7. The implications of this for employment are manifold and profound.

First and foremost, the Digital Revolution has ushered in new job sectors and roles that were previously unimaginable. From app developers to social media managers, digital marketers to data analysts, the job market has expanded to include a plethora of digital roles that require not only technical proficiency but also a new set of soft skills, including digital literacy, adaptability, and continuous learning.

Moreover, the rise of digital platforms has revolutionized the traditional job search and recruitment processes. Platforms like LinkedIn, Indeed, and remote work websites have become the new norm for job hunting, enabling employers and job seekers to connect in ways that were previously impossible. This digital job marketplace is more dynamic and competitive, requiring job seekers to develop robust digital footprints and personal brands to stand out.

The Digital Revolution has also been a catalyst for the gig economy, a labor market characterized by the prevalence of short-term contracts or freelance work as opposed to permanent jobs. Digital platforms such as Upwork, Freelancer, and Fiverr have facilitated this shift, providing a marketplace for gig work that spans across industries and borders. This shift towards gig work represents a significant change in the traditional employment contract, with implications for job security, work-life balance, and the social safety net.

Remote work, another byproduct of the Digital Revolution, has become increasingly viable and popular, thanks in part to advancements in communication technology. Tools like Zoom, Slack, and Asana have made it possible for teams to collaborate effectively from anywhere in the world, challenging the traditional notion that productive work can only happen within the confines of an office. The recent global events have only accelerated this trend, making remote work a new normal for many industries.

However, the Digital Revolution is not without its challenges. The rapid pace of technological change has led to a skills gap, with many workers finding their skills obsolete in the face of new digital tools and technologies. This has highlighted the need for continuous education and upskilling, underscoring the importance of lifelong learning as a critical component of career development in the digital age.

Furthermore, the automation of tasks through AI and machine learning raises questions about the future of work and the potential displacement of jobs. While automation can increase efficiency and create new opportunities, it also poses the risk of job loss in sectors where tasks can be automated. Navigating this landscape requires a nuanced understanding of how technology complements human skills and how workers can adapt to coexist with AI.

In conclusion, the Digital Revolution has irrevocably altered the job market, creating new opportunities and challenges alike. As we move forward, it's crucial to embrace the changes brought about by this revolution, leveraging the power of digital technology to enhance our work lives and career paths. This era of digital transformation calls for a proactive approach to career development, one that emphasizes adaptability, continuous learning, and the strategic use of digital tools to navigate the ever-evolving job market. In this context, the role of guidance, such as that provided in "Innovative Jobscapes," becomes invaluable, offering insights and strategies to thrive in the digital age.

Chapter 2: The New Age of Job Hunting

Beyond Traditional Job Searches

In the realm of modern employment, venturing *beyond traditional job searches* is not just an option; it's a necessity. Gone are the days when securing a job was a straightforward path, defined by newspaper ads, direct applications, and a handful of interviews. The digital era has ushered in a paradigm shift, transforming the very landscape of how job seekers connect with potential employers and uncover opportunities.

This evolution is not merely about changing platforms—from print to digital—but about a fundamental shift in strategies, mindsets, and the tools at our disposal. Traditional job searches were often reactive, with candidates responding to advertised vacancies. Today, the proactive job seeker must navigate a multitude of channels, leveraging technology not just to find jobs, but to create opportunities where none seem to exist.

Networking has always been a cornerstone of job searching, but its form and function have been revolutionized by digital platforms. Social media sites like LinkedIn, Twitter, and even Facebook have become vital arenas for professional networking. These platforms allow for the building of professional relationships, sharing of industry insights, and direct engagement with companies and thought leaders. The art of networking now involves curating a digital presence that reflects one's professional brand, contributing valuable content, and engaging in meaningful conversations online.

Personal branding is another critical component of modern job searching. In a sea of candidates, defining and differentiating oneself is crucial. This involves a strategic presentation of one's skills, experiences, and professional ethos across various online platforms. A well-crafted LinkedIn profile, a professional blog, or a portfolio website can serve as dynamic resumes, showcasing not just what one has done, but who one is as a professional.

The rise of the **gig economy** has also expanded the horizons of job searching. Platforms like Upwork, Freelancer, and Fiverr offer a marketplace for skills, where job seekers can find short-term engagements or freelance projects. This not only provides a source of income but also an opportunity to build a portfolio, gain diverse experience, and establish a network of professional contacts.

Remote work opportunities have further broadened the scope of job searching. With companies increasingly open to hiring remote employees, job seekers are no longer confined by geographical boundaries. Platforms like We Work Remotely, Remote.co, and FlexJobs specialize in remote and flexible job listings, opening up a global job market.

The concept of **'creating your own job'** through entrepreneurship or intrapreneurship has gained traction. With the democratization of access to resources and information, starting a business or pitching an innovative project within one's current company has become more feasible than ever. This approach requires not just a keen sense of the market and a viable idea but also the ability to brand and market oneself effectively.

In navigating these new terrains, **upskilling** and **reskilling** have become essential. The digital economy values not just academic qualifications but a continuous learning mindset. Online learning platforms like Coursera, Udemy, and LinkedIn Learning offer courses that can help job seekers stay abreast of industry trends, acquire new skills, and enhance their employability in a rapidly changing job market.

As we delve into this new age of job hunting, it's clear that the strategies of yesterday are no longer sufficient. The job seekers who thrive are those who embrace the full spectrum of opportunities that the digital age offers. They are the ones who understand that job searching is no longer about simply finding a vacancy but about creating a professional identity, building a network, continuously learning, and sometimes, creating the opportunities themselves.

In sharing these insights, the aim is not just to highlight the challenges of the modern job market but to illuminate the pathways that lead to opportunities. It's about empowering you, the reader, to navigate these innovative jobscapes with confidence, creativity, and a proactive spirit.

Leveraging Technology for Employment Opportunities

In the current landscape of the job market, the strategic **leveraging of technology** has become an indispensable tool for uncovering and seizing employment opportunities. This evolution represents a significant departure from traditional job search methodologies, propelling us into a realm where digital platforms, artificial intelligence, and global connectivity redefine the rules of engagement.

The advent of the **digital age** has democratized access to information and opportunities, making the job search process more dynamic and interconnected. Job seekers now have at their disposal a vast array of digital tools and platforms designed to optimize the job search process, from online job boards and company career pages to professional networking sites and social media platforms. These resources offer not only a broader range of opportunities but also the ability to connect directly with potential employers and key industry players.

Online job boards and **career websites**, such as Indeed, Monster, and Glassdoor, serve as comprehensive repositories of job listings, providing users with the ability to filter opportunities by industry, job function, location, and more. These platforms often offer additional resources, including company reviews, salary benchmarks, and career advice, further aiding job seekers in making informed decisions.

Professional networking sites, most notably LinkedIn, have transformed the landscape of professional connections and job searching. LinkedIn, in particular, allows individuals to showcase their professional profile, build and engage with their network, and access job listings directly through the platform. The power of LinkedIn lies not only in its job listings but also in its ability to facilitate connections, endorsements, and introductions, effectively enabling users to tap into the hidden job market.

The role of **social media** in job searching has also expanded, with platforms like Twitter and Facebook increasingly being used for professional networking and job searching. Companies often use these platforms to share job openings, industry news, and insights into company culture, providing job seekers with a more holistic view of potential employers.

The emergence of **niche job search websites** and apps tailored to specific industries or types of work further exemplifies the customization and specialization afforded by technology. Platforms like AngelList for startups, Behance for creative professionals, and Stack Overflow for developers cater to specific professional communities, offering targeted job listings and networking opportunities.

Applicant Tracking Systems (ATS) have become a standard tool for employers in managing job applications. Understanding the intricacies of ATS and optimizing resumes and applications for these systems is crucial for job seekers to ensure their applications are seen by human eyes. This involves using relevant keywords, clear formatting, and strategic content placement to improve visibility and compatibility with ATS algorithms.

The rise of **freelance and remote work platforms** such as Upwork, Freelancer, and Remote.co reflects the growing trend towards gig work and telecommuting. These platforms connect freelancers with projects and positions that can be performed remotely, offering flexibility and diversity in employment opportunities.

In this digital era, **personal branding** has taken on new importance. Establishing a strong online presence, whether through a personal website, blog, or social media profiles, allows individuals to showcase their skills, experiences, and professional interests. This digital footprint becomes a key component of the job search strategy, providing a platform for job seekers to articulate their value proposition and engage with potential employers and collaborators.

Moreover, **technological upskilling** platforms like Coursera, Udemy, and LinkedIn Learning have made it easier for job seekers to acquire new skills or enhance existing ones. These platforms offer courses and certifications in a wide range of subjects, from data analysis and coding to digital marketing and project management, enabling individuals to stay competitive in a rapidly evolving job market.

In navigating the digital terrain of job searching, it's clear that technology is not just a facilitator but a catalyst for new opportunities. It requires job seekers to adopt a more proactive, strategic approach to their job search, leveraging digital tools and platforms to not only find opportunities but to connect, engage, and stand out in a crowded market. As we delve deeper into this digital era, the potential to leverage technology for employment opportunities is boundless, limited only by one's ability to adapt, innovate, and embrace the digital revolution.

Chapter 3: Digital Networking and Personal Branding

The Power of Social Media in Job Hunting

In today's digital era, the power of social media in job hunting cannot be overstated. It has revolutionized the way we connect, communicate, and even the way we present ourselves professionally. As we navigate through the vast landscapes of employment opportunities, social media stands out as a beacon, illuminating paths that were once hidden and opening doors to opportunities that were previously unimaginable.

Social media platforms, once primarily used for personal connections and entertainment, have transformed into robust professional networks. LinkedIn, with its 700+ million users, is at the forefront of this revolution, serving not just as a digital resume but as a dynamic platform for professional networking, personal branding, and job searching. Here, professionals can showcase their skills, achievements, and expertise, connect with like-minded individuals, join industry-specific groups, and engage with potential employers.

But the influence of social media extends beyond LinkedIn. Twitter, for example, offers a more informal yet potent avenue for job seekers. By following industry leaders, participating in relevant conversations, and sharing insightful content, individuals can build their professional reputation and network. Twitter chats, often organized around specific hashtags, provide a platform for real-time engagement with professionals across various fields, offering insights, advice, and even job leads.

Facebook, with its vast user base, has also carved out a space for professional networking through industry-specific groups and company pages. Joining these groups and engaging in discussions can provide valuable information about job openings, company cultures, and industry trends. Additionally, Facebook's Marketplace and job listing features have become valuable tools for local job searches.

Instagram, primarily known for its visual content, has emerged as an unlikely yet effective tool for personal branding and networking. Creative professionals, in particular, can leverage Instagram to showcase their portfolios, share their creative process, and connect with potential employers and clients. The use of industry-related hashtags can significantly increase visibility, attracting the attention of recruiters and companies looking for talent.

The power of social media in job hunting also lies in its ability to provide insights into company cultures and values. Many companies use social media to share news, achievements, and aspects of their workplace culture, offering a glimpse into what it's like to work for them. This information can be invaluable for job seekers, helping them align their applications with the company's values and culture, and tailor their approach to stand out.

Moreover, social media platforms have become essential tools for learning and professional development. LinkedIn Learning, for example, offers a wide range of courses and tutorials, allowing individuals to upskill and stay current with industry trends. Similarly, following thought leaders and industry influencers can provide a continuous stream of valuable content, from articles and blog posts to webinars and podcasts, further enhancing one's knowledge and expertise.

However, the power of social media comes with a caveat. The digital footprint we leave behind can significantly impact our professional reputation. Therefore, it's crucial to curate one's online presence carefully, ensuring that public profiles reflect professionalism, expertise, and the value one can bring to potential employers.

In harnessing the power of social media for job hunting, it's essential to be strategic, authentic, and proactive. Building a strong professional network, engaging in meaningful conversations, and continuously learning and adapting are key to leveraging social media effectively. As we explore the innovative jobscapes of today, social media stands as a pivotal tool, not just in finding opportunities but in creating them, marking a new era in the pursuit of career advancement and fulfillment.

Building a Personal Brand Online

In the digital age, **building a personal brand online** has transcended mere trend status to become a fundamental career strategy. This is not just about crafting an online persona; it's about articulating your unique value proposition, establishing your professional credibility, and differentiating yourself in a crowded marketplace. As we delve into the nuances of constructing a robust online presence, it becomes clear that a well-defined personal brand is a powerful tool in navigating the innovative jobscapes of today.

The cornerstone of building an effective online brand is **clarity**. This begins with a deep introspection about who you are as a professional, what you stand for, and where your strengths lie. It's about honing in on your unique skills, experiences, and the value you bring to the table. Once clarity is achieved, articulating your brand across various online platforms becomes a more streamlined and impactful process.

LinkedIn, as the preeminent professional networking site, serves as the foundation of most online personal branding efforts. A compelling LinkedIn profile goes beyond a static resume to tell a cohesive story of your professional journey. This includes a well-crafted summary that encapsulates your professional identity, detailed descriptions of your work experiences that highlight your contributions and achievements, and a thoughtful curation of skills and endorsements that reinforce your expertise. Regularly publishing articles, sharing insightful content, and engaging in meaningful discussions can further augment your presence, positioning you as a thought leader in your field.

Beyond LinkedIn, leveraging other social media platforms like **Twitter**, **Instagram**, and **Facebook** can amplify your personal brand. Each platform offers unique opportunities to showcase different facets of your professional identity. For instance, Twitter is an excellent platform for sharing industry news, engaging with thought leaders, and participating in real-time discussions. Instagram, with its visual-centric format, can be particularly effective for creative professionals to showcase their portfolios or give glimpses into their creative process.

Meanwhile, Facebook's groups and community features can be instrumental in connecting with like-minded professionals and industry-specific communities.

Creating a **personal website or blog** is another powerful dimension of building an online brand. A personal website provides a centralized hub for your professional narrative, offering the flexibility to showcase your portfolio, share your bio, blog about industry insights, and even host a personal vlog. It's a space entirely under your control, free from the constraints of social media platforms, allowing for deeper storytelling and personal expression.

Content creation is the engine that drives personal branding online. Whether it's writing articles, producing videos, crafting infographics, or simply sharing insightful commentary, content is what engages your audience and showcases your expertise. Consistency is key; regular updates keep your audience engaged and help maintain your relevance in the digital landscape.

Engagement is the other side of the content coin. Building a brand isn't just about broadcasting your achievements and insights; it's also about listening, responding, and participating in a broader conversation. This means commenting on others' posts, answering questions, and being an active member of online communities. Engagement not only increases your visibility but also helps in building relationships and expanding your professional network.

Navigating the realm of online personal branding also requires a keen awareness of **digital etiquette and privacy**. It's essential to maintain professionalism across all platforms, be mindful of the content you share, and understand privacy settings to control who sees what. Remember, every tweet, post, or comment contributes to the mosaic of your online brand.

In the journey of building a personal brand online, it's crucial to remember that authenticity is the bedrock of all efforts. Authenticity resonates; it's what connects you with your audience, fosters trust, and solidifies your professional reputation. As you craft and curate your online presence, let your genuine self shine through, for it's your uniqueness that sets you apart in the vast digital expanse.

In essence, building a personal brand online is about strategically harnessing the power of digital platforms to tell your professional story, connect with opportunities, and engage with a global community. It's a dynamic, ongoing process that, when done right, opens doors to new career horizons and positions you as a key player in the innovative jobscapes of the future.

Chapter 4: The Gig Economy and Freelancing

Navigating the World of Short-Term Engagements

In the vast expanse of today's job market, the rise of **short-term engagements** stands out as a significant trend, reshaping traditional employment models. This shift towards gig work, freelance projects, and contract roles is not just a fleeting change but a fundamental evolution in how we perceive and engage with work. As we delve into this dynamic segment of the employment landscape, it becomes evident that navigating the world of short-term engagements requires a nuanced understanding, strategic approach, and an adaptable mindset.

The allure of short-term engagements lies in their flexibility, diversity, and the opportunity for professionals to curate a varied career portfolio. These roles can range from freelance writing and graphic design projects to consulting gigs and interim leadership positions. Each engagement serves as a stepping stone, allowing professionals to build a mosaic of experiences that enhance their skills, expand their networks, and deepen their industry insights.

Understanding the Gig Economy: At the heart of short-term engagements is the gig economy, characterized by its on-demand, project-based work structure. Platforms like **Upwork, Freelancer**, and **Fiverr** have become the digital marketplaces for gigs, connecting freelancers with clients across the globe. Navigating these platforms requires more than just signing up; it demands a strategic profile setup, a compelling portfolio, and a keen sense of how to pitch one's services effectively.

Building a Freelance Brand: Success in short-term engagements often hinges on one's ability to market themselves. Building a strong personal brand becomes crucial. This involves not just showcasing your skills and past work but also articulating your unique value proposition. Social media platforms, personal websites, and online portfolios play a pivotal role in this branding effort, serving as platforms to share your work, gather testimonials, and engage with your professional community.

Networking and Relationship Building: While short-term engagements may lack the long-term security of traditional roles, they offer unparalleled opportunities for networking. Each project is a chance to impress and build lasting relationships with clients, who can become repeat customers or refer you to new opportunities. Engaging with professional groups, both online and offline, and staying connected with past clients can turn sporadic gigs into a steady stream of opportunities.

Skill Development and Adaptability: The transient nature of short-term engagements necessitates a commitment to continuous learning and adaptability. The gig economy thrives on current trends and emerging skills. Professionals must stay abreast of industry developments, investing in upskilling and reskilling to remain competitive. Online learning platforms, workshops, and webinars are invaluable resources for keeping skills sharp and relevant.

Financial and Legal Considerations: Navigating short-term engagements also involves understanding the financial and legal aspects of freelancing. This includes setting competitive yet fair rates, managing irregular income streams, and understanding contractual agreements. It's also prudent to be aware of tax implications and to consider setting up a legal entity for your freelance business, ensuring that you're protected and professional in all transactions.

Work-Life Balance: While the flexibility of short-term engagements is appealing, it also poses challenges to work-life balance. Freelancers and gig workers must be adept at managing their time, setting clear boundaries, and ensuring that the freedom of gig work doesn't blur the lines between personal and professional life too much.

In the journey through the world of short-term engagements, resilience, networking, and a proactive approach to career development are key. Each project, no matter how small, is an opportunity to learn, grow, and build towards a fulfilling career. As we navigate this landscape, we embrace the diversity of experiences it offers, crafting careers that are not only varied and vibrant but also rich with opportunities for personal and professional growth.

In essence, short-term engagements represent more than just a shift in employment models; they signify a broader transformation in our relationship with work. They challenge us to be more entrepreneurial, to take ownership of our career paths, and to find value in the journey as much as the destination. As we explore these dynamic jobscapes, we are not just participants but pioneers, charting new territories in the ever-evolving world of work.

Strategies for Success in Freelancing

Embarking on a freelance career is akin to navigating an uncharted sea; it's full of potential rewards but also rife with challenges. The freedom and flexibility of freelancing are counterbalanced by the need for self-discipline, perseverance, and strategic planning. To thrive in this dynamic environment, it's essential to adopt a multifaceted approach, combining skill development, marketing acumen, and a robust support network.

1. Cultivating a Niche: Specialization can be a powerful differentiator in the crowded freelance market. By honing your skills in a specific area, you become more attractive to clients looking for experts. Whether it's graphic design, copywriting, web development, or digital marketing, excelling in a niche not only allows you to command higher rates but also helps in building a strong brand identity.

2. Portfolio Development: Your portfolio is the linchpin of your freelance business. It should not only showcase your best work but also reflect the breadth and depth of your skills. A well-curated portfolio that's easily accessible online can significantly enhance your visibility and attract potential clients. Including case studies or testimonials that demonstrate the impact of your work can further bolster your portfolio's effectiveness.

3. Continuous Learning and Skill Enhancement: The freelance world is ever-evolving, with new tools, technologies, and best practices emerging regularly. Staying abreast of these changes and continuously upgrading your skills is crucial.

Leveraging online learning platforms, attending workshops, and participating in industry conferences can keep you at the cutting edge of your field.

4. Strategic Networking: Building a robust professional network is invaluable in freelancing. Networking isn't just about attending events; it's about fostering genuine relationships with peers, mentors, and potential clients. Online communities, social media platforms, and professional associations can be fertile grounds for expanding your network. Remember, a strong network can lead to referrals, collaborations, and new opportunities.

5. Effective Marketing and Self-Promotion: As a freelancer, you are your own brand, and effective marketing is key to your success. This involves more than just a strong online presence; it's about communicating your value proposition clearly and compellingly. Utilizing social media, blogging, email marketing, and even speaking engagements can help in building your visibility and establishing your expertise in your field.

6. Mastering Client Relations: Building and maintaining positive relationships with clients is fundamental to freelance success. This includes clear communication, setting realistic expectations, delivering high-quality work on time, and being open to feedback. Happy clients are not only more likely to return but also to recommend your services to others.

7. Financial Management: Navigating the financial aspects of freelancing, from setting competitive rates to managing irregular income streams, requires careful planning. Creating a budget, setting aside money for taxes, and investing in a good invoicing and accounting system can help in maintaining financial stability. Additionally, building an emergency fund can provide a buffer during lean periods.

8. Balancing Work and Life: One of the biggest challenges in freelancing is finding a healthy work-life balance. Without the structure of a traditional job, it's easy to either overwork or struggle with productivity. Setting a regular schedule, creating a dedicated workspace, and taking time off for rest and rejuvenation are crucial for long-term sustainability.

9. Embracing Innovation and Adaptability: The freelance landscape is characterized by rapid changes and unpredictability. Embracing this fluidity, being open to new ideas, and adapting your strategies accordingly can open up new avenues for growth and success.

10. Building Resilience: Finally, resilience is perhaps the most critical attribute for a freelancer. Rejection, project droughts, and challenging clients are part and parcel of the freelance journey. Developing a thick skin, learning from setbacks, and staying committed to your goals are essential for overcoming these hurdles.

In essence, thriving as a freelancer requires a blend of professional excellence, strategic marketing, and personal resilience. It's about continuously evolving, leveraging your unique skills, and creating value that resonates with your clients. As you navigate the freelancing world, remember that each project, each client, and each challenge is a stepping stone towards building a fulfilling and prosperous freelance career.

Chapter 5: Remote Work: The New Frontier

Embracing the Global Workspace

In the evolving narrative of modern employment, the concept of a global workspace stands out as a transformative force, reshaping not just where we work, but how we connect, collaborate, and create value across borders. This global convergence, powered by digital technology, has dismantled traditional geographical and cultural barriers, ushering in an era of unprecedented connectivity and opportunity.

The Digital Infrastructure: At the core of this global workspace is a robust digital infrastructure that facilitates seamless communication and collaboration. Cloud-based platforms, video conferencing tools, and project management software have become the new bedrock of global work, enabling teams to synchronize and operate as cohesive units, irrespective of their physical locations. Tools like **Zoom, Slack, Asana,** and **Trello** have become indispensable, not just for their functionality, but for their role in fostering a connected, inclusive work environment.

Cultural Competency and Diversity: Embracing the global workspace also necessitates a deep appreciation for cultural diversity and an adeptness at navigating the nuances of cross-cultural communication. The richness of a globally diverse team lies in its varied perspectives, which can spur creativity and innovation. However, it also requires an understanding and respect for differences in communication styles, work ethics, and business etiquettes. Developing cultural competency—through training, open dialogue, and immersive experiences—becomes key to harnessing the full potential of a global team.

Flexible Work Models: The shift towards a global workspace has catalyzed the adoption of more flexible work models. Remote work, once a perk, has now become a norm in many sectors, supported by policies that emphasize results over rigid schedules. This flexibility has opened up global talent pools, allowing companies to tap into a wider array of skills and expertise, while also offering professionals the freedom to work from anywhere, thereby achieving a better work-life balance.

Leveraging Global Talent Networks: In this borderless workspace, building and nurturing a global professional network has become more feasible and valuable than ever. Platforms like LinkedIn have transcended their role as networking sites to become global marketplaces for talent, ideas, and opportunities. Engaging with these networks, participating in global forums, and contributing to international projects can significantly amplify one's professional reach and impact.

Language and Communication Skills: Effective communication is the linchpin of global collaboration. While English often serves as a lingua franca in international business, learning additional languages can provide a competitive edge, deepen cultural understanding, and foster stronger relationships. Moreover, honing soft skills, such as active listening, empathy, and clear articulation, becomes crucial in navigating the nuances of global communication.

Adapting to Time Zones: One of the practical challenges of a global workspace is managing across different time zones. This requires not just logistical coordination but also sensitivity to the personal lives and schedules of team members. Adopting asynchronous work methods, setting clear expectations around availability, and using time zone management tools can help mitigate these challenges, ensuring productivity and well-being.

Ethical and Sustainable Practices: As businesses operate on a global scale, their impact—social, environmental, and economic—also amplifies. Embracing a global workspace thus carries with it a responsibility to adhere to ethical practices, respect local laws and customs, and contribute positively to the communities and environments where they operate. Sustainability becomes not just a corporate mandate but a shared value that guides decision-making and operations across geographies.

Continuous Learning and Innovation: Finally, thriving in a global workspace demands a commitment to continuous learning and innovation. The rapid pace of change, coupled with the diverse challenges and opportunities presented by global work, necessitates a mindset of growth, adaptability, and curiosity. Staying informed about global trends, emerging technologies, and best practices in international business can equip professionals with the knowledge and skills to navigate this complex landscape successfully.

In embracing the global workspace, we are not just expanding our professional horizons; we are participating in a larger movement towards a more interconnected, innovative, and inclusive world of work. It's a journey that challenges us to grow, adapt, and reimagine what's possible, offering a vista of opportunities that are as boundless as the global landscape itself.

Tools and Best Practices for Remote Employment

In the tapestry of modern employment, remote work has emerged as a pivotal thread, weaving together flexibility, technology, and the global workforce into a vibrant new paradigm. As we navigate this realm, it becomes crucial to arm ourselves with the right tools and adopt best practices that ensure productivity, collaboration, and work-life harmony. The journey into remote employment is as much about leveraging technology as it is about redefining workplace culture and personal work habits.

Optimizing Your Digital Toolbox: The foundation of effective remote work lies in a robust digital toolkit designed to facilitate communication, project management, and task execution. Platforms like **Slack** or **Microsoft Teams** have become the virtual watercooler, fostering real-time conversations, team meetings, and even casual catch-ups. For project and task management, tools like **Asana**, **Trello**, and **Monday.com** offer intuitive interfaces for tracking progress, assigning tasks, and setting deadlines, ensuring that everyone is aligned and accountable.

The Power of Cloud Computing: Cloud-based services, including **Google Workspace** and **Microsoft 365**, allow for seamless file sharing, collaboration, and storage, making it possible for team members to work on documents simultaneously, regardless of their physical location. This collaborative approach not only streamlines workflows but also promotes a sense of unity and shared purpose among remote teams.

Mastering Video Conferencing: Video conferencing tools like **Zoom, Skype**, and **Google Meet** have become indispensable in the remote work era, enabling face-to-face interactions that are crucial for maintaining team cohesion and facilitating complex discussions. However, video conferencing etiquette is key—ensuring a stable internet connection, using headphones to minimize background noise, and being mindful of video and audio settings can significantly enhance the meeting experience for everyone involved.

Cybersecurity Measures: With the shift to remote work, cybersecurity becomes paramount. Employing VPNs (Virtual Private Networks), using strong, unique passwords, and ensuring that antivirus and firewall software are up-to-date are essential practices to protect sensitive data and maintain the integrity of remote work environments.

Creating a Conducive Work Environment: Beyond digital tools, creating a physical workspace that is conducive to productivity is vital. This means setting up a dedicated work area, investing in ergonomic furniture, and ensuring proper lighting. The goal is to create a space that not only minimizes distractions but also promotes focus and well-being.

Structured Schedules and Clear Boundaries: One of the challenges of remote work is the blurring of lines between professional and personal life. Establishing a structured daily routine, setting clear work hours, and communicating these boundaries to family and housemates can help in maintaining a healthy work-life balance. Regular breaks and scheduled downtime are also crucial to prevent burnout and sustain productivity over the long term.

Fostering Team Culture and Engagement: Maintaining a strong team culture remotely requires intentional effort. Regular virtual team-building activities, celebrating milestones, and encouraging informal interactions can help in nurturing connections and reinforcing a sense of belonging. Recognition programs and open channels for feedback also contribute to a positive and inclusive remote work culture.

Continuous Learning and Adaptation: The landscape of remote work is continuously evolving, necessitating an attitude of lifelong learning and flexibility. Staying informed about new tools, technologies, and remote work trends can provide fresh insights and strategies to enhance the remote work experience.

Emphasizing Communication and Transparency: Clear, consistent communication is the lifeline of remote teams. This involves not only regular updates and check-ins but also being transparent about challenges and setbacks. Encouraging open dialogue and fostering an environment where team members feel comfortable sharing their thoughts and concerns is crucial for collaborative problem-solving and innovation.

In embracing remote employment, we're not just adapting to a new way of working; we're participating in a broader shift towards a more flexible, inclusive, and connected global workforce. By integrating the right tools with best practices that prioritize productivity, well-being, and community, we can navigate this landscape with confidence, unlocking new possibilities for collaboration, creativity, and work-life harmony in the process.

Chapter 6: AI and Automation: Friends or Foes?

Understanding AI's Role in Job Creation and Displacement

In the intricate tapestry of the modern job market, Artificial Intelligence (AI) emerges as a dual-edged sword, wielding the power to both create new opportunities and displace traditional roles. As we delve into the complexities of AI's impact, it becomes evident that this technological force is not just reshaping industries but also redefining the very essence of work. The journey to comprehend AI's role in job creation and displacement requires a nuanced exploration of its applications, implications, and the strategies we must adopt to navigate this evolving landscape.

The Genesis of AI in the Workplace: AI's integration into the workplace marks a significant evolution from rudimentary automation to sophisticated systems capable of learning, reasoning, and decision-making. From chatbots enhancing customer service to predictive analytics in finance, AI's applications are as diverse as they are transformative. This technological leap forward promises efficiency, precision, and scalability, yet it also raises critical questions about the future of human labor.

AI-Driven Job Creation: Contrary to the dystopian view of AI as a job destroyer, this technology is also a potent job creator. The emergence of AI has catalyzed the growth of entirely new sectors and professions. Roles such as AI ethicists, data scientists, and machine learning engineers are in high demand, reflecting the need for human oversight, creativity, and strategic thinking in leveraging AI technologies. Moreover, AI's capacity to analyze vast datasets and identify trends can spur innovation, leading to the development of new products, services, and business models.

The Displacement Dilemma: While AI opens new avenues for employment, it also poses a significant risk of displacement, particularly for roles characterized by repetitive tasks and routine decision-making. Industries such as manufacturing, retail, and transportation are witnessing a paradigm shift, where automation and AI-driven systems are increasingly assuming tasks traditionally performed by humans. This displacement is not just confined to low-skilled jobs; even professions such as legal analysis, journalism, and certain aspects of healthcare are feeling the impact of AI's encroachment.

Navigating the AI Landscape: Understanding AI's dual role in the job market is the first step in navigating its challenges and opportunities. Education and skill development emerge as critical strategies in this context. Emphasizing STEM education, fostering digital literacy, and promoting continuous learning are essential to equip the workforce with the skills needed to thrive in an AI-driven economy.

The Importance of Soft Skills: In an environment where many technical tasks are automated, soft skills such as creativity, emotional intelligence, problem-solving, and adaptability become increasingly valuable. These inherently human attributes are beyond the current capabilities of AI, highlighting the importance of roles that require complex human interactions, empathy, and ethical judgment.

Ethical Considerations and AI Governance: As AI becomes more pervasive, ethical considerations and governance frameworks become paramount. Issues such as bias in AI algorithms, privacy concerns, and the ethical use of AI underscore the need for comprehensive policies and guidelines to ensure that AI technologies are developed and deployed responsibly, with a focus on societal welfare and equitable distribution of benefits.

Collaboration Between Humans and AI: The future of work is not a zero-sum game between humans and AI but rather a collaborative endeavor. Augmented intelligence, where AI tools enhance human capabilities, is a burgeoning area. By automating routine aspects of jobs, AI can free up individuals to focus on more strategic, creative, and interpersonal tasks, thereby enriching job roles and making work more fulfilling.

The Path Forward: Embracing AI in the job market requires a proactive approach, characterized by policy innovation, corporate responsibility, and individual adaptability. Governments and organizations must invest in education, retraining programs, and social safety nets to ease the transition for displaced workers. At the same time, individuals must take ownership of their lifelong learning journey, continuously updating their skills to remain relevant in an ever-changing job landscape.

In sum, AI's role in job creation and displacement is a multifaceted phenomenon that presents both challenges and opportunities. By understanding the nuances of AI's impact, fostering a culture of continuous learning, and emphasizing the irreplaceable value of human creativity and empathy, we can navigate the complexities of this new era. In doing so, we not only safeguard our place in the future of work but also harness AI's potential to enhance the quality of work and life, creating a more innovative, inclusive, and prosperous job landscape.

Adapting to an Automated Work Environment

In the labyrinth of modern employment, the surge of automation represents both a challenge and a catalyst for transformation. The narrative of work is being rewritten under the influence of automation, compelling us to reassess our roles, skills, and strategies for career advancement. As we navigate this automated work environment, the emphasis shifts from mere adaptation to proactive engagement with the technologies that are reshaping our professional landscapes.

Embracing Technological Fluency: At the forefront of adapting to automation is the pursuit of technological fluency. This entails not just a familiarity with digital tools and platforms but a deeper understanding of how automation technologies work and their implications for our roles. Whether it's learning the basics of coding, understanding data analytics, or getting acquainted with AI and machine learning concepts, enhancing our tech fluency empowers us to work alongside automated systems effectively.

Redefining Human Value: As tasks become increasingly automated, the value we bring as professionals evolves. Our focus turns to inherently human skills that automation cannot replicate— critical thinking, creativity, empathy, and complex problem-solving. Cultivating these skills becomes paramount, ensuring that we complement rather than compete with automated systems. This shift underscores the importance of roles that require a human touch, from customer service and client relations to strategic planning and innovation.

Agile and Continuous Learning: The rapid pace of technological change necessitates a mindset of agile and continuous learning. Staying abreast of industry trends, emerging technologies, and new methodologies is essential to remain relevant. This might involve regular upskilling through online courses, workshops, and webinars, or even pursuing more formal education to deepen one's expertise in areas less susceptible to automation.

Flexibility and Adaptability: Automation introduces a dynamic element to work processes, often leading to rapid changes in job responsibilities and workflows. Cultivating flexibility and adaptability becomes crucial, allowing us to pivot when our tasks evolve or when we're required to interface with new automated systems. This adaptability extends to our willingness to embrace new work models, including remote work, flexible schedules, and project-based roles, which are becoming increasingly prevalent in automated environments.

Collaborative Working with Automated Systems: As automated systems become more integrated into our work environments, developing the skills to collaborate effectively with these systems is essential. This involves understanding the capabilities and limitations of automation tools, learning to interpret and use the data they generate, and effectively managing the interface between human and machine tasks.

Ethical Considerations and Critical Evaluation: With the rise of automation comes a host of ethical considerations, from data privacy concerns to the potential for bias in automated decisions. Developing a critical lens through which to evaluate the ethical implications of automated systems is vital. This includes advocating for transparency, accountability, and fairness in the design and implementation of automation technologies.

Networking and Community Engagement: In an automated work environment, professional networks and communities play a pivotal role in navigating career paths. Engaging with peers, joining professional associations, and participating in industry forums can provide insights into how others are adapting to automation, offering new perspectives and opportunities for collaboration.

Personal Well-being and Resilience: Finally, adapting to an automated work environment requires attention to personal well-being and resilience. The uncertainties and rapid changes associated with automation can be stressful, making it essential to develop strategies for managing stress, maintaining work-life balance, and building resilience to navigate the challenges and opportunities that automation brings.

In essence, adapting to an automated work environment is a multifaceted endeavor that requires us to evolve as professionals continually. By embracing technological fluency, focusing on inherently human skills, committing to lifelong learning, and fostering adaptability, we can not only navigate the challenges of automation but also seize the opportunities it presents. In doing so, we open the door to new possibilities for innovation, collaboration, and personal growth in the ever-changing landscape of modern employment.

Chapter 7: Upskilling and Reskilling for the Future

Identifying Skills for Tomorrow's Jobs

In the ever-evolving narrative of the modern employment landscape, the ability to identify and cultivate the skills necessary for tomorrow's jobs is paramount. As we stand at the confluence of technological advancements, shifting economic paradigms, and emerging global challenges, the question of which skills will be most valuable looms large. The future of work is not just about adapting to change; it's about anticipating it, shaping it, and being prepared to thrive within it.

The Foundation of Future Skills: At the heart of future-ready skills lies a combination of adaptability, technological literacy, and a deep-rooted commitment to lifelong learning. The rapid pace of change in today's world means that the skills that are in demand today may evolve or become obsolete tomorrow. Therefore, the ability to learn, unlearn, and relearn is not just an asset but a necessity.

Technological Proficiency: In an era where digital transformation is ubiquitous, technological proficiency emerges as a critical skill set. This encompasses not only the ability to use existing digital tools but also the understanding of emerging technologies such as artificial intelligence, blockchain, and the Internet of Things (IoT). Familiarity with these technologies, even at a basic level, can provide a significant advantage in a job market that increasingly values tech-savvy professionals.

Critical Thinking and Problem-Solving: As automation and AI take over routine tasks, the human capacity for critical thinking, complex problem-solving, and creative innovation becomes more valuable. Employers are looking for individuals who can navigate ambiguity, think strategically, and devise innovative solutions to complex challenges. These skills are applicable across industries and job functions, making them essential for future-proofing one's career.

Emotional Intelligence and Interpersonal Skills: The importance of emotional intelligence and interpersonal skills is magnified in a world where automation and virtual communication are prevalent. The ability to empathize, collaborate effectively, and build relationships is crucial in fostering teamwork, leadership, and customer engagement. These "soft skills" complement technical abilities and are often the differentiator in leadership and client-facing roles.

Data Literacy: In a data-driven world, the ability to interpret, analyze, and leverage data is increasingly critical. Data literacy goes beyond mere statistical knowledge; it involves understanding how data can inform decisions, drive strategies, and create value. This skill is becoming indispensable across sectors, from marketing and finance to healthcare and public policy.

Sustainability and Ethical Leadership: As global challenges such as climate change and social inequality become more pressing, skills related to sustainability and ethical leadership gain prominence. Professionals who can drive sustainable practices, ethical decision-making, and social responsibility within organizations are in demand. This reflects a broader shift towards values-driven business models and the role of corporations in addressing global issues.

Global Competency and Cultural Agility: The interconnected nature of today's world requires a workforce that is globally competent and culturally agile. This means being able to work effectively across cultures, languages, and geographies, and understanding the global implications of local actions. As businesses expand their global footprint, professionals with these skills will be crucial for navigating international markets and multicultural teams.

Entrepreneurial Mindset: An entrepreneurial mindset, characterized by innovation, risk-taking, and resilience, is valuable even for those not looking to start their own ventures. Organizations are increasingly seeking intrapreneurs who can drive innovation from within, challenging the status quo and spearheading new initiatives.

Navigating the Future of Work: Identifying and developing these skills requires a proactive approach to career development. This involves staying informed about industry trends, seeking out learning opportunities, and being open to new experiences. Mentorship, networking, and continuous feedback are also vital in aligning one's skill set with the evolving demands of the job market.

In essence, the skills for tomorrow's jobs are as diverse as they are dynamic, blending technical proficiency with critical soft skills, a global perspective, and a commitment to ethical and sustainable practices. By identifying and cultivating these skills, we not only prepare ourselves for the future of work but also contribute to shaping a more resilient, innovative, and inclusive job landscape.

Lifelong Learning as a Career Strategy

In the kaleidoscope of today's rapidly evolving job landscape, lifelong learning emerges not just as a concept but as a critical career strategy. This commitment to continuous education and skill development is pivotal in navigating the shifting sands of employment opportunities shaped by technological advancements, globalization, and changing economic tides. As we delve into the essence of lifelong learning, it's clear that this journey is about more than acquiring knowledge; it's about cultivating a mindset geared towards growth, adaptability, and resilience.

The Imperative of Continuous Upskilling: In an era where the half-life of skills is shrinking, the importance of continuous upskilling cannot be overstated. The rapid pace of technological innovation means that what is relevant today may become obsolete tomorrow. Embracing a culture of continuous learning is essential to stay ahead of the curve. This involves not only formal education but also informal learning avenues such as workshops, webinars, online courses, and even self-directed learning through reading, experimentation, and practical application.

The Role of Digital Platforms in Learning: The digital revolution has democratized access to education, making it possible to learn virtually anything, anytime, anywhere. Platforms like **Coursera, edX, Udacity**, and **LinkedIn Learning** offer a plethora of courses ranging from technical skills in coding and data analysis to soft skills in leadership and communication. These platforms also provide micro-credentials and certifications that can enhance a resume and demonstrate commitment to professional growth.

Adaptability and the Growth Mindset: Lifelong learning is as much about adaptability and mindset as it is about acquiring specific skills. Cultivating a growth mindset, a term coined by psychologist Carol Dweck, involves embracing challenges, persisting in the face of setbacks, and viewing effort as a path to mastery. This mindset is crucial for adapting to new roles, technologies, and industries.

Networking and Collaborative Learning: Learning is inherently social, and the exchange of ideas, knowledge, and experiences enriches the learning process. Professional networks, both online and offline, provide invaluable opportunities for collaborative learning. Engaging with peers, mentors, and industry leaders can offer new insights, expose you to different perspectives, and open doors to unexpected opportunities.

Personal Learning Projects and Experimentation: Hands-on experience is a powerful learning tool. Undertaking personal projects, whether developing a new software application, starting a blog, or even launching a side business, can provide practical learning experiences that build skills and confidence. These projects not only enhance learning but can also become portfolio pieces that showcase your skills to potential employers.

The Integration of Learning into Daily Life: Making learning an integral part of daily life ensures that it becomes a habit rather than a chore. This can involve setting aside dedicated time for learning, integrating educational podcasts into your commute, or even engaging in learning challenges with peers to maintain motivation.

Learning Agility: Learning agility, the ability to rapidly learn, unlearn, and relearn, is a key competency in the modern workplace. This agility enables professionals to pivot when industries change, roles evolve, or new technologies emerge. It's about being able to apply lessons from one context to another and continuously evolving your skill set in response to new challenges.

Reflective Practice and Self-Assessment: Lifelong learning also involves regular self-assessment and reflective practice. This means taking stock of your skills, understanding your strengths and areas for improvement, and setting targeted learning goals. Reflection enhances the learning process, ensuring that it is intentional and aligned with your career aspirations.

In essence, lifelong learning as a career strategy is about embracing a proactive, curious, and flexible approach to professional development. It's about recognizing that in a world of constant change, the pursuit of knowledge and skills is an ongoing journey, not a destination. By committing to lifelong learning, we not only enrich our careers but also open ourselves to a world of possibilities, ready to adapt, grow, and thrive in the innovative jobscapes of the future.

Chapter 8: Entrepreneurship in the Digital Age

Turning Innovative Ideas into Business Realities

In the dynamic terrain of today's job market, the ability to transform innovative ideas into tangible business realities stands as a beacon for aspiring entrepreneurs and change-makers. This journey, marked by creativity, resilience, and strategic foresight, is not merely about launching a new product or service; it's about ushering in solutions that address unmet needs, disrupt traditional industries, and create value in unprecedented ways. As we delve into the intricacies of this process, it becomes evident that turning ideas into realities involves a multifaceted approach, blending vision with practicality, and passion with pragmatism.

Cultivating a Culture of Innovation: The genesis of any groundbreaking business reality begins with fostering a culture of innovation. This entails creating an environment where curiosity is encouraged, risks are embraced as learning opportunities, and failure is viewed as a stepping stone to success. Encouraging diverse perspectives, promoting cross-disciplinary collaboration, and providing a safe space for experimentation are essential to nurturing the creative thinking that fuels innovation.

Market Research and Validation: Transforming an idea into a business reality requires a deep understanding of the market landscape. Conducting thorough market research to identify target demographics, understand customer pain points, and assess competitive offerings is crucial. Validation involves engaging with potential customers through surveys, focus groups, and prototypes to gather feedback and refine the concept, ensuring that the solution aligns with market needs and preferences.

Building a Solid Business Model: A viable business model is the backbone of any successful venture. This framework outlines how the business will create, deliver, and capture value. Key components include defining the value proposition, identifying revenue streams, determining cost structures, and establishing key partnerships. The goal is to create a sustainable model that balances innovation with economic viability.

Leveraging Technology and Digital Tools: In the digital age, technology plays a pivotal role in bringing innovative ideas to life. Leveraging digital tools and platforms can enhance product development, streamline operations, and facilitate customer engagement. Whether it's utilizing cloud computing for scalability, harnessing data analytics for insights, or employing social media for marketing, technology is a powerful enabler for new ventures.

Securing Funding and Resources: Turning an idea into reality often requires capital and resources. Exploring various funding options, from bootstrapping and crowdfunding to angel investors and venture capital, is essential to fuel growth. Crafting a compelling pitch, showcasing the potential for impact and return on investment, and building a strong network of supporters can increase the chances of securing the necessary backing.

Building a Strong Team: Behind every successful venture is a team that shares the vision and possesses complementary skills. Building a team that encompasses a range of expertise, from product development and marketing to finance and operations, is crucial. Fostering a culture of open communication, continuous learning, and shared goals can drive the team to turn the vision into reality.

Iterative Development and Agile Methodologies: The path from idea to business reality is rarely linear. Adopting an iterative approach, characterized by rapid prototyping, continuous testing, and agile methodologies, allows for flexibility and adaptability. This iterative cycle of building, measuring, and learning facilitates ongoing improvement and responsiveness to market feedback.

Navigating Regulatory and Legal Landscapes: Understanding and navigating the regulatory and legal aspects of establishing a business is critical. This includes securing the necessary licenses, protecting intellectual property, and ensuring compliance with industry standards and regulations. Seeking legal counsel and advice can mitigate risks and lay a strong foundation for the business.

Launching and Scaling: Successfully launching the business involves strategic planning, effective marketing, and meticulous execution. Building brand awareness, engaging with customers, and delivering exceptional value are key to gaining traction. As the business grows, scaling operations, expanding the product or service offering, and exploring new markets become the next frontiers.

In essence, turning innovative ideas into business realities is a complex yet rewarding journey that demands a blend of creativity, strategic thinking, and perseverance. By embracing a holistic approach that spans ideation to execution, entrepreneurs can navigate the challenges and seize the opportunities that lie in transforming vision into value. In doing so, they not only contribute to the evolving jobscapes but also pave the way for a future where innovation drives progress, prosperity, and positive change.

The Essentials of Starting Your Own Venture

Embarking on the journey to start your own venture is akin to navigating uncharted waters, where the thrill of discovery coexists with the challenges of the unknown. As we delve into this endeavor, it's imperative to recognize that the essence of entrepreneurship transcends mere business creation; it's about bringing a vision to life, solving real-world problems, and making a tangible impact. This journey, while fraught with uncertainties, is also ripe with opportunities for innovation, growth, and self-discovery.

Crafting a Vision and Identifying Your Niche: The genesis of any successful venture lies in a clear, compelling vision coupled with a well-defined niche. This vision serves as the north star, guiding every strategic decision and action. Identifying a niche involves a deep understanding of market needs, pain points, and gaps that your venture can uniquely address. This phase requires meticulous research, introspection, and a keen eye for opportunities that align with your skills, passions, and the value you aim to deliver.

Developing a Robust Business Plan: A comprehensive business plan is the blueprint of your venture, outlining your business model, market strategy, financial projections, and operational framework. This document is not just a roadmap for your entrepreneurial journey but also a crucial tool for communicating your vision to potential investors, partners, and stakeholders. It should articulate your value proposition, target market, competitive landscape, revenue streams, and growth strategies with clarity and precision.

Securing Funding and Managing Finances: Financing your venture is a critical hurdle that can determine its viability and scalability. Exploring various funding sources, from bootstrapping and crowdfunding to angel investors and venture capital, requires a strategic approach tailored to your venture's stage, industry, and financial needs. Effective financial management, including budgeting, cash flow management, and financial forecasting, is essential to sustain operations, fuel growth, and navigate financial challenges.

Building a Talented, Committed Team: Behind every successful venture is a team that shares the founder's vision and brings diverse skills, perspectives, and expertise to the table. Assembling this team involves not just hiring for skill but also for cultural fit, shared values, and a mutual commitment to the venture's mission. Fostering a culture of collaboration, innovation, and continuous learning is crucial for team cohesion, motivation, and performance.

Leveraging Technology and Digital Tools: In today's digital age, technology is a critical enabler for startups. From cloud computing and data analytics to social media and e-commerce platforms, leveraging the right technologies can enhance operational efficiency, customer engagement, and market reach. Staying abreast of technological trends and adopting a tech-savvy approach can provide a competitive edge and drive business innovation.

Establishing a Strong Brand and Marketing Presence: Building a strong brand and a compelling marketing strategy is pivotal in creating visibility, credibility, and customer loyalty. This involves crafting a unique brand identity, delivering consistent messaging across all touchpoints, and employing a mix of marketing channels tailored to your target audience. Content marketing, social media engagement, SEO, and influencer partnerships are key tactics to build brand awareness and drive customer acquisition.

Navigating Legal and Regulatory Frameworks: Understanding and complying with legal and regulatory requirements is fundamental to avoid pitfalls and safeguard your venture. This includes registering your business, securing the necessary licenses and permits, protecting intellectual property, and adhering to industry-specific regulations. Seeking legal counsel and staying informed about legal obligations can mitigate risks and ensure smooth operations.

Embracing Agility and Resilience: The entrepreneurial journey is inherently dynamic, often requiring pivots, adaptations, and resilience in the face of setbacks. Embracing agility, being open to feedback, and learning from failures are key to navigating challenges, seizing opportunities, and fostering continuous improvement.

In essence, starting your own venture is a multifaceted endeavor that demands vision, strategy, and unwavering determination. By adhering to these essentials, entrepreneurs can navigate the complexities of building a business, overcome the inevitable obstacles, and ultimately, turn their innovative ideas into thriving realities. In this journey, the rewards extend beyond financial gains, encompassing personal growth, the satisfaction of making a difference, and the legacy of creating something enduring and impactful.

Chapter 9: The Future of Workplaces and Cultures

Predicting Changes in Work Environments

In the vast expanse of the evolving employment landscape, predicting changes in work environments is akin to charting a course through the shifting sands of innovation, societal shifts, and economic fluctuations. As we stand on the precipice of this new era, it's imperative to gaze into the crystal ball of the future workspaces, understanding that the only constant in this journey is change itself. The work environments of tomorrow are being sculpted by a confluence of forces, from groundbreaking technological advancements to a redefined ethos of work-life integration, each playing a pivotal role in reshaping the contours of our professional lives.

The Digital Transformation Acceleration: At the forefront of this evolution is the relentless pace of digital transformation. Technologies such as artificial intelligence (AI), machine learning, the Internet of Things (IoT), and blockchain are not just buzzwords but the architects of the future workplace. These technologies are streamlining operations, automating routine tasks, and opening new avenues for innovation, thereby fundamentally altering the nature of work. The future work environment is one where digital fluency is not just an asset but a necessity, compelling professionals to continuously hone their digital skills to remain relevant.

The Rise of Remote and Hybrid Work Models: The recent global shifts have catapulted remote work from a niche perk to a mainstream mode of operation. This trend is set to continue, with hybrid models— blending remote work with traditional office settings—becoming the norm. This shift is not merely about where we work but how work is structured, managed, and evaluated, emphasizing outcomes over hours and productivity over presence. The future work environment is characterized by flexibility, autonomy, and a focus on work-life harmony, challenging the traditional 9-to-5 paradigm.

The Emergence of Gig Economy and Freelancing: The gig economy is reshaping the employer-employee dynamic, fostering a marketplace where short-term contracts or freelance work replace traditional long-term employment. This shift towards project-based work is empowering professionals to tailor their careers to their lifestyles, skills, and aspirations, offering unprecedented flexibility but also necessitating a proactive approach to career development, networking, and personal branding.

Sustainability and Social Responsibility: The growing emphasis on sustainability and corporate social responsibility (CSR) is influencing work environments, pushing businesses to adopt practices that are not only economically viable but also environmentally sound and socially responsible. Future workplaces are increasingly being judged by their impact on the planet and society, with sustainability becoming a core component of corporate identity and operations.

The Evolving Office Space: The physical workspace is undergoing a transformation, moving away from the traditional cubicle-laden landscapes to more dynamic, collaborative, and adaptable spaces. Co-working spaces, shared offices, and innovation hubs are becoming more prevalent, designed to foster collaboration, creativity, and community. These spaces are equipped with the latest technology, ergonomic design, and wellness facilities, reflecting a holistic approach to the work environment.

Lifelong Learning and Skills Development: The rapid pace of change necessitates a culture of lifelong learning within work environments. Organizations are increasingly investing in learning and development programs, recognizing that the upskilling and reskilling of their workforce is critical for staying competitive. The future workplace is one that provides continuous learning opportunities, encouraging employees to grow their skill sets and adapt to the evolving demands of their roles.

The Importance of Diversity, Equity, and Inclusion (DEI): The future work environment is unequivocally inclusive, embracing diversity in all its forms. The recognition of the value that diverse perspectives bring to problem-solving, innovation, and decision-making is driving companies to build more inclusive cultures. This involves not only diverse hiring practices but also the creation of supportive, equitable environments where every employee can thrive.

Mental Health and Well-being: The acknowledgment of the importance of mental health and well-being is reshaping work environments, with companies increasingly adopting policies and practices that support employee wellness. From flexible working hours and wellness programs to mental health days and supportive management practices, the future workplace prioritizes the holistic well-being of its employees.

Predicting changes in work environments requires us to navigate the confluence of technology, culture, and societal values. As we venture into this new era, it's clear that the work environments of the future will be fluid, dynamic, and centered around the principles of flexibility, innovation, and inclusivity. In embracing these changes, we not only adapt to the future but actively shape it, creating workspaces that foster growth, well-being, and a profound sense of purpose.

Fostering Inclusive and Dynamic Work Cultures

In the tapestry of today's evolving employment paradigm, the cultivation of inclusive and dynamic work cultures stands as a cornerstone of organizational success. This endeavor transcends traditional workplace norms, weaving together diversity, equity, inclusivity, and agility into the very fabric of organizational DNA. As we embark on this journey, it becomes evident that fostering such environments is not merely a policy initiative but a strategic imperative that drives innovation, resilience, and sustainable growth.

Embracing Diversity as a Strength: The foundation of an inclusive work culture lies in the recognition and celebration of diversity in all its forms—gender, ethnicity, age, sexual orientation, disability, and thought. Understanding that diverse teams bring a plethora of perspectives to the table is crucial. These varied viewpoints catalyze creativity, enhance problem-solving, and lead to more robust decision-making processes. It's about creating a workspace where differences are not just tolerated but valued as a source of strength and innovation.

Equity and Accessibility: True inclusivity demands equity—ensuring that every member has access to the same opportunities, resources, and support to succeed. This involves dismantling systemic barriers, creating equitable hiring practices, and providing tailored support mechanisms that acknowledge and address the unique challenges faced by underrepresented groups. It's about leveling the playing field so that talent, not background or circumstance, dictates one's trajectory.

Building a Culture of Belonging: An inclusive work culture fosters a sense of belonging, where every individual feels seen, heard, and valued. This is cultivated through transparent communication, empathetic leadership, and policies that prioritize employee well-being and work-life harmony. Initiatives such as mentorship programs, employee resource groups, and regular feedback channels can enhance the sense of community and belonging within the organization.

Promoting Psychological Safety: A dynamic work culture is one where employees feel psychologically safe to express ideas, raise concerns, and challenge the status quo without fear of retribution. This environment encourages risk-taking, learning from failures, and open dialogue, which are essential for innovation and growth. Leaders play a pivotal role in modeling this behavior, creating a space where vulnerability is seen as a strength, not a weakness.

Agility and Adaptability: The ability to pivot in response to changing market dynamics, technological advancements, and evolving customer needs is a hallmark of a dynamic work culture. This agility is fostered by flat organizational structures, cross-functional teams, and a project-based approach that allows for flexibility and rapid response to change. Empowering employees to make decisions, experiment with new ideas, and lead initiatives fosters a proactive and adaptable workforce.

Continuous Learning and Development: In a landscape characterized by perpetual change, fostering a culture of continuous learning and development is paramount. Providing employees with opportunities for upskilling, reskilling, and personal growth ensures that the workforce remains competitive and aligned with the organization's evolving needs. This can be achieved through training programs, learning platforms, and a culture that celebrates curiosity and lifelong learning.

Sustainable Practices and Corporate Social Responsibility: An inclusive and dynamic work culture also recognizes the organization's role in the broader community and ecosystem. Implementing sustainable practices, engaging in corporate social responsibility initiatives, and adopting ethical business practices reflect a commitment to not just organizational success but also societal and environmental well-being.

Measuring and Evolving: Cultivating an inclusive and dynamic work culture is an ongoing process that requires regular assessment, reflection, and adaptation. Utilizing metrics to gauge diversity, employee engagement, and inclusivity, and soliciting regular feedback from employees, can provide insights into areas of strength and opportunities for improvement. It's a journey of continuous evolution, driven by a commitment to creating work environments where everyone can thrive.

In essence, fostering inclusive and dynamic work cultures is about more than policies and programs—it's about embedding these values into the very essence of how an organization operates. It's a strategic imperative that not only enhances employee satisfaction and retention but also drives innovation, adaptability, and long-term success. In these nurturing environments, individuals are empowered to reach their full potential, contributing to a collective future where diversity, creativity, and resilience are the keys to navigating the new frontiers of employment.

Chapter 10: Case Studies: Success Stories in Innovation

Real-Life Examples of Innovative Job Hunting and Employment

In navigating the ever-evolving job market, innovative approaches to job hunting and employment have emerged, showcasing resilience, creativity, and adaptability. These real-life examples illuminate paths less traveled, where individuals have harnessed the power of technology, networking, and strategic thinking to carve out unique career opportunities, reshaping traditional notions of employment in the process.

Leveraging Social Media for Personal Branding: Take the story of Emily, a graphic designer who transformed her career prospects by utilizing Instagram to showcase her portfolio. By curating a visually compelling feed that highlighted her design skills, creativity, and unique aesthetic, Emily attracted the attention of potential employers and clients. Her proactive approach to social media turned her profile into a dynamic portfolio, leading to freelance opportunities, collaborations, and eventually, a full-time position at a leading design firm.

Utilizing LinkedIn for Thought Leadership:
John, a software engineer, leveraged LinkedIn not just as a networking platform but as a space for sharing industry insights, technical tutorials, and commentary on emerging technologies. By consistently posting valuable content, engaging with other professionals, and contributing to discussions, John established himself as a thought leader in his field. This visibility opened doors to speaking engagements, consulting opportunities, and a pivotal role at a tech startup looking for an expert with not only technical acumen but also industry influence.

Crowdsourcing Opportunities through Twitter:
Sarah, a marketing professional, tapped into the power of Twitter to uncover hidden job opportunities. By actively engaging with industry influencers, participating in relevant hashtag conversations, and sharing her insights on marketing trends, Sarah caught the eye of a startup founder looking for a marketing lead. This connection, initiated through a tweet, led to a conversation, an interview, and ultimately, a job offer that aligned perfectly with Sarah's skills and career aspirations.

Creating a Niche Blog to Attract Opportunities:
Alex, an environmental scientist passionate about sustainable living, started a blog to share research, tips, and personal experiments in reducing waste. Over time, the blog gained a substantial following, positioning Alex as a subject matter expert in

sustainability. This platform not only allowed Alex to connect with like-minded individuals but also attracted the attention of organizations looking for consultants and speakers on sustainability, leading to numerous opportunities for collaboration and employment.

Developing an Online Course as a Career Launchpad: Sofia, an expert in data analytics, created an online course to teach others the fundamentals of data analysis using a popular software tool. The course, hosted on an educational platform, garnered thousands of students, showcasing Sofia's expertise and teaching ability. This endeavor not only provided a passive income stream but also led to Sofia being recognized by a tech company in need of a data analytics trainer for their team, resulting in a lucrative consultancy role.

Participating in Hackathons for Visibility and Opportunities: Michael, a software developer, regularly participated in hackathons and coding competitions, often sharing his projects and achievements on his personal blog and social media. These participations not only honed his skills but also showcased his problem-solving ability and creativity to a wider audience. A tech company, impressed by Michael's innovative solutions at a hackathon, reached out with an offer to join their R&D team, recognizing the value he could bring to their innovation efforts.

Networking through Virtual Conferences: In the wake of global shifts towards virtual events, Lisa, a project manager, maximized her participation in virtual conferences by engaging actively in sessions, asking insightful questions, and connecting with speakers and attendees through the event platforms. Her proactive approach led to meaningful connections, mentorship opportunities, and eventually, a job offer from a company that valued her enthusiasm for continuous learning and her ability to engage with industry leaders and trends.

These stories exemplify the myriad ways in which individuals are redefining job hunting and employment, leveraging digital platforms, personal projects, and strategic networking to create opportunities that align with their skills, passions, and career goals. These innovative approaches underscore the importance of adaptability, continuous learning, and the willingness to explore unconventional paths in carving out a fulfilling and dynamic career in today's job market.

Conclusion: Charting Your Path in Innovative Jobscapes

Preparing for the Unpredictable Future of Work

As we stand at the crossroads of a rapidly transforming employment landscape, preparing for the unpredictable future of work becomes not just an endeavor but a necessity. The horizon of our professional futures is being reshaped by forces that are as dynamic as they are diverse: technological breakthroughs, demographic shifts, global connectivity, and a growing emphasis on sustainability and social impact. In this ever-evolving scenario, the key to not only surviving but thriving lies in our ability to anticipate, adapt, and innovate.

Embracing a Mindset of Lifelong Learning: The bedrock of future-proofing your career is a steadfast commitment to continuous education and skill development. The notion that learning ends upon graduation is obsolete in a world where new technologies and methodologies emerge at breakneck speed. Cultivating a love for learning and a curiosity that transcends traditional boundaries is essential. This might mean enrolling in online courses, attending workshops and seminars, or simply dedicating time each day to read, explore, and satisfy your intellectual curiosity.

Cultivating Adaptability and Resilience: The future of work demands not just technical skills but also a high degree of emotional intelligence, adaptability, and resilience. The ability to navigate change, bounce back from setbacks, and pivot in response to new opportunities is invaluable. This involves developing a positive attitude towards failure as a learning experience, being open to feedback, and being willing to step out of your comfort zone to tackle new challenges.

Leveraging Technology and Digital Literacy: In an era dominated by AI, machine learning, and big data, digital literacy goes beyond basic proficiency in software tools. It encompasses an understanding of how technology impacts your field, the ability to work alongside intelligent systems, and a strategic approach to leveraging digital tools to enhance productivity and innovation. Staying abreast of technological trends and understanding their implications for your industry and role is crucial.

Building a Robust Professional Network: In the interconnected world of work, your network is your net worth. Building and nurturing a diverse professional network can open doors to opportunities that you might not have otherwise encountered. This involves engaging with your industry community, both online and offline, participating in professional groups, and contributing to conversations and projects. Remember, networking is not just about what you can get but also about what you can give back to your community.

Fostering Creativity and Innovation: The ability to think creatively and innovate is increasingly becoming a differentiator in the job market. This involves looking at problems from new angles, questioning the status quo, and being open to experimenting with new ideas. Cultivating an environment, both personally and professionally, that encourages creativity and values innovation is key to staying relevant in the future job market.

Prioritizing Health and Well-being: Recognizing the importance of physical and mental well-being is crucial in preparing for the future of work. The demands of modern work can often lead to burnout if not managed properly. Prioritizing self-care, maintaining a healthy work-life balance, and developing stress management techniques are essential for sustaining a long and fulfilling career.

Advocating for Flexibility and Work-Life Harmony: The future of work is not just about what we do but also how we do it. Advocating for flexible work arrangements, remote work options, and policies that support work-life harmony is becoming increasingly important. This involves not only seeking out employers who value these principles but also embodying them in your work and advocating for them within your workplace.

Engaging in Meaningful Work: More than ever, professionals are seeking work that is not only financially rewarding but also personally fulfilling and socially impactful. Aligning your career with your values, passions, and the causes you care about can lead to greater job satisfaction and a sense of purpose. This might mean seeking employers whose mission aligns with your own, engaging in volunteer work, or even starting your own venture that addresses a social or environmental issue.

Preparing for the unpredictable future of work is a multifaceted journey that requires a proactive, strategic approach. It's about continuously evolving, both personally and professionally, to meet the demands of a changing world. By embracing lifelong learning, cultivating adaptability, leveraging technology, and striving for meaningful engagement in our work, we can navigate the uncertainties of the future with confidence and optimism. This preparation not only positions us to seize emerging opportunities but also enables us to play an active role in shaping the future of work itself.

Embracing Change with Optimism and Strategy

In the labyrinth of modern employment, change is not just a constant but a catalyst for growth and innovation. As we navigate through the shifting sands of the job market, the ability to embrace change with both optimism and a well-crafted strategy becomes paramount. This journey is less about predicting the future with precision and more about equipping ourselves with the tools, mindset, and resilience to adapt to whatever lies ahead.

Cultivating an Optimistic Outlook: The first step in embracing change is fostering a fundamentally optimistic outlook towards the future. It's about seeing change not as a harbinger of uncertainty but as a doorway to new opportunities. This mindset is grounded in the belief that every disruption brings with it the seeds of growth and renewal. By maintaining a positive outlook, we can better navigate the emotional landscape of change, turning potential anxiety into proactive enthusiasm.

Strategic Planning and Goal Setting: While optimism fuels our drive, a clear strategy gives direction to our journey. Strategic planning in the context of an unpredictable job market involves setting flexible goals that can adapt to changing circumstances. It's about identifying your core competencies, understanding the evolving needs of your industry, and aligning your career trajectory with these dynamics. Setting SMART (Specific, Measurable, Achievable, Relevant, Time-bound) goals can provide clarity and focus, even in times of flux.

Emphasizing Skill Agility: In a landscape where the half-life of skills is rapidly shrinking, skill agility – the ability to learn, unlearn, and relearn – becomes crucial. This means staying abreast of emerging trends in your field, investing in continuous learning, and not shying away from acquiring entirely new skill sets. The future belongs to those who can pivot their expertise to where the demand is, be it mastering new technologies, adapting to new business models, or embracing new ways of working.

Building a Resilient Mindset: Resilience, the ability to bounce back from setbacks and challenges, is at the heart of navigating change successfully. This involves developing coping mechanisms for stress, cultivating a strong support network, and viewing failures as stepping stones rather than roadblocks. Resilience is what enables us to keep moving forward, even when the path is uncertain.

Leveraging Your Network: In times of change, your network can be both a safety net and a springboard to new opportunities. Cultivating a diverse and supportive professional network ensures you have access to advice, mentorship, and insights that can help you navigate career transitions. It's also about being a valuable contributor to your network, sharing your knowledge, and supporting others in their journeys.

Adopting a Proactive Approach to Change: Waiting for change to happen to you can leave you reactive and unprepared. Instead, adopting a proactive approach means actively seeking out new opportunities, anticipating industry shifts, and positioning yourself at the forefront of change. This could mean volunteering for new projects, proposing innovative solutions, or even changing career paths to align with future trends.

Mindfulness and Adaptability: In the face of change, maintaining a sense of mindfulness can help us stay grounded and focused. It's about being fully present in the moment, accepting change as it comes, and adapting with grace. Mindfulness practices can help reduce stress, enhance focus, and improve our capacity to adapt to new situations.

Charting Your Own Path: Ultimately, embracing change with optimism and strategy is about charting your own path through the uncharted territories of the future job market. It's about defining success on your own terms, staying true to your values, and pursuing work that is not only rewarding but also meaningful.

As we stand on the brink of a new era in employment, the call to embrace change has never been more urgent or more promising. Armed with optimism, a strategic approach, and a toolkit of adaptable skills, we can turn the unpredictability of the future into a landscape of limitless possibilities. This journey is not just about navigating the new frontiers of employment; it's about shaping them, with every step we take, into a world where work is not just a means to an end but a platform for growth, creativity, and fulfillment.

Appendices

Useful Resources for Innovative Job Hunters

In the quest to navigate the ever-evolving employment landscape, arming oneself with a robust arsenal of resources is key. As we delve into this chapter, let's explore an array of indispensable tools and platforms that stand as beacons for those seeking to carve out their niche in the modern job market. These resources are not merely aids; they are catalysts for transformation, empowerment, and success in the digital age.

LinkedIn: The quintessential professional networking platform, LinkedIn transcends its function as a digital resume repository to become a dynamic hub for career development. It offers unparalleled access to industry insights, professional networking opportunities, and a wealth of job listings tailored to your skills and aspirations. Engaging with LinkedIn Learning can also bolster your skill set with courses ranging from data analytics to creative thinking.

Glassdoor: Offering a transparent look into company cultures, salaries, and interview processes, Glassdoor empowers job seekers with the information needed to make informed decisions. Its extensive database of company reviews and salary reports can be instrumental in negotiating your next role.

Indeed: As one of the most comprehensive job search engines, Indeed aggregates listings from myriad sources, making it a one-stop-shop for job hunters. Its user-friendly interface and personalized job alerts simplify the search process, making job hunting less daunting.

Coursera & edX: Lifelong learning is the cornerstone of career resilience. Platforms like Coursera and edX offer courses from top universities and institutions worldwide, covering a vast array of subjects. Whether you're looking to upskill in data science, delve into digital marketing, or explore entrepreneurship, these platforms provide the tools to stay competitive.

Remote.co & We Work Remotely: For those venturing into the realm of remote work, these platforms are invaluable. They not only list remote job opportunities but also offer insights into the remote work culture, helping you navigate the nuances of virtual employment.

Meetup: Networking remains a potent tool in the job seeker's kit. Meetup allows you to find and join groups with similar professional interests, providing a platform for in-person or virtual gatherings. These connections can often lead to job opportunities, partnerships, or valuable industry insights.

Canva: In the digital age, personal branding is paramount. Canva offers a user-friendly design platform to create visually compelling resumes, portfolios, and social media content that can help you stand out in a crowded job market.

Feedly & Pocket: Staying informed about industry trends is crucial. Feedly and Pocket allow you to curate content from your favorite publications, blogs, and news sources, ensuring you're always in the loop about the latest developments in your field.

Slack Communities: Slack is not just for team communication. It hosts myriad communities where professionals can share knowledge, ask questions, and network. Joining Slack channels related to your industry can provide insider access to job openings and freelance opportunities.

AngelList: For those drawn to the startup world, AngelList provides a platform to discover job openings in startups at various stages. It's an excellent resource for finding roles in innovative companies poised to shape the future.

Mentorship Platforms (MentorCruise, ADPList): Finding a mentor can accelerate your career growth. Platforms like MentorCruise and

ADPList connect you with experienced professionals in your industry who can provide guidance, feedback, and support.

Google Alerts: Setting up Google Alerts for specific job titles, companies, or industry news can ensure you're the first to know about relevant opportunities and developments.

In the digital era, the job hunt is no longer confined to the classifieds section of a newspaper. It's a dynamic, multifaceted endeavor that spans the digital expanse. By leveraging these resources, you can navigate the job market with confidence, equipped with the knowledge, skills, and connections to thrive in the new frontiers of employment. Remember, the journey to your dream job is not a solitary trek but a voyage best navigated with the right tools and a community of fellow travelers and guides.

Glossary of Terms

In the realm of **Innovative Jobscapes**, the language we use is pivotal. It not only conveys ideas but also shapes our understanding of the evolving employment landscape. As we traverse this new terrain, let's demystify some key terms that are foundational to our journey.

Artificial Intelligence (AI): The simulation of human intelligence in machines that are programmed to think and learn like humans. In the context of employment, AI can both augment and automate job tasks, leading to shifts in job requirements and creation of new roles.

Blockchain: A decentralized digital ledger technology known for its secure and transparent way of recording transactions. Beyond cryptocurrencies, blockchain has implications for secure and verifiable professional credentials, potentially transforming hiring processes.

Coworking Spaces: Shared work environments used by individuals who are self-employed or working for different employers, fostering community and collaboration among diverse professionals.

Digital Nomad: Individuals who leverage telecommunications technologies to earn a living and conduct their life in a nomadic manner, often working remotely from foreign countries, coffee shops, public libraries, and co-working spaces.

Freelancing: The act of working on a per-job or per-task basis, often for multiple clients, as opposed to being employed by a single company. The gig economy has significantly expanded freelancing opportunities across various sectors.

Gig Economy: A labor market characterized by the prevalence of short-term contracts or freelance work as opposed to permanent jobs. It's driven by companies operating under a "share economy" model, such as Uber and Airbnb.

LinkedIn Learning: An online educational platform that offers courses taught by industry experts in software, creative, and business skills to help individuals pursue their personal and professional goals.

MOOCs (Massive Open Online Courses): Free online courses available for anyone to enroll, offering a flexible way to learn new skills and advance career prospects. Platforms like Coursera, edX, and Udacity are popular providers of MOOCs.

Personal Branding: The practice of marketing oneself and one's career as brands. It involves establishing a prescribed image or impression in the mind of others about an individual.

Remote Work: A working style that allows professionals to work outside of a traditional office environment, based on the concept that work does not need to be done in a specific place to be executed successfully.

SEO (Search Engine Optimization): The practice of increasing the quantity and quality of traffic to your website through organic search engine results, crucial for personal branding and online visibility.

Soft Skills: Personal attributes that enable someone to interact effectively and harmoniously with other people, including communication, problem-solving, and teamwork skills, increasingly valued in the modern workplace.

STEM (Science, Technology, Engineering, and Mathematics): An educational and professional field focused on hard sciences and technical skills, critical in driving innovation and economic growth.

Telecommuting: Working from a remote location outside of a corporate office, often from home, leveraging technology to stay connected with colleagues and work processes.

Upskilling: The process of learning new or advanced skills to enhance one's ability to perform in the workplace, particularly important in an era where technological advancements rapidly change job requirements.

Virtual Teams: Groups of people who work together from different geographic locations and rely on communication technology such as email, video or voice conferencing, and social media to collaborate.

This glossary serves as a compass, guiding us through the intricate web of concepts that define the contemporary employment ecosystem. By familiarizing ourselves with these terms, we not only enhance our vocabulary but also deepen our understanding of the forces shaping our professional destinies in this digital age.

About the Author

Morgan E. Blake stands at the forefront of a transformative era in the world of employment and career development. Operating under a veil of anonymity, this decision to publish under the pseudonym Morgan E. Blake is more than a mere preference for privacy; it is a deliberate choice to ensure the content speaks louder than the persona, allowing the insights to resonate on their merit in the intricate tapestry of job markets and career strategies.

With a foundation built on **extensive research** and **practical experience**, Morgan's expertise spans the dynamic spectrum of evolving employment trends. This depth of knowledge is not confined to the theoretical; it is enriched by a wealth of real-world applications, offering **guidance and wisdom** that transcend conventional boundaries and appeal to a broad audience across various professional landscapes.

Morgan's journey into the realm of employment and career development was not a serendipitous one; it was a path marked by a keen observation of the **seismic shifts** brought about by technological advancements and the globalization of work cultures. Recognizing the growing obsolescence of traditional job-hunting methods, Morgan embarked on a mission to chart a new course, one that navigates the complexities of the contemporary job market with **innovation and foresight**.

"Innovative Jobscapes: Navigating New Frontiers in Employment" is more than a book; it is Morgan E. Blake's manifesto for the modern job seeker, entrepreneur, and career changer. It encapsulates a vision for the future of work, where traditional paradigms are challenged, and new opportunities are embraced with **optimism and strategy**. Each chapter is a testament to Morgan's dedication to equipping readers with the tools and knowledge necessary to thrive in an ever-changing professional environment.

Morgan's approach to writing and research is characterized by a **captivating and credible language**, making complex concepts not only accessible but deeply relatable. The narrative is interspersed with real-life success stories, serving as beacons of inspiration for those poised on the brink of their next professional venture.

In the end, Morgan E. Blake is not just an author; he is a visionary and a guide, offering a window into the future of employment, where innovation paves the way to new and exhilarating frontiers. With "Innovative Jobscapes," Morgan invites readers to embark on a journey, one that promises not just insight and information but a new perspective on the possibilities that lie ahead in the world of work.

Summary

www.ingramcontent.com/pod-product-compliance
Lightning Source LLC
Chambersburg PA
CBHW071054290526
45795CB00004B/1491